Gospel Light's SonWest ROUNDUP

A RIP-ROARING GOOD TIME WITH JESUS! VBS

Vacation Bible School

Join the stampede!

Gospel Light's SonWest ROUNDUP

A RIP-ROARING GOOD TIME WITH JESUS! VBS

Vacation Bible School

Join the stampede!

© 2013 Gospel Light, Ventura, CA 93006. All rights reserved. Printed in the U.S.A.
ISBN 10 0-8307-6473-9   ISBN 13 978-0-8307-6473-0   gospellightvbs.com

Vacation Bible School

Join the stampede!

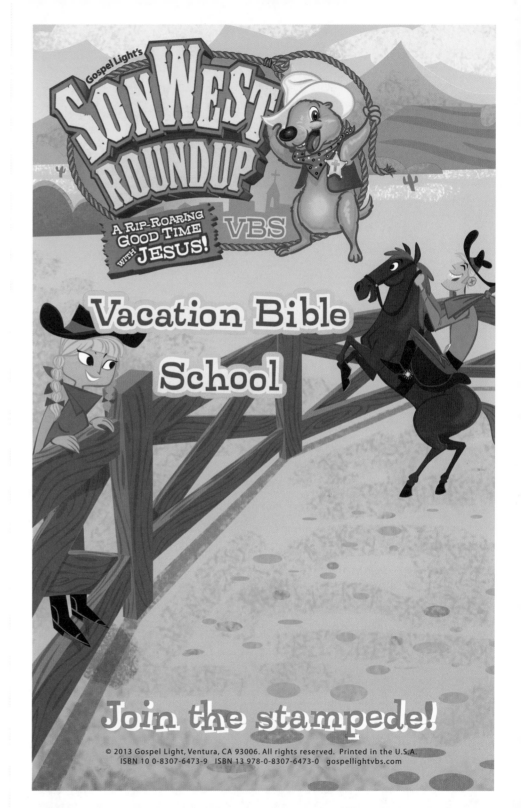

Vacation Bible School

Join the stampede!

© 2013 Gospel Light, Ventura, CA 93006. All rights reserved. Printed in the U.S.A.
ISBN 10 0-8307-6473-9 ISBN 13 978-0-8307-6473-0 gospellightvbs.com

SonWest ROUNDUP

A RIP-ROARING GOOD TIME WITH JESUS! VBS

Gospel Light's

Vacation Bible School

Join the stampede!

Gospel Light's

SonWest ROUNDUP

A RIP-ROARING GOOD TIME WITH JESUS! VBS

Vacation Bible School

Join the stampede!

© 2013 Gospel Light, Ventura, CA 93006. All rights reserved. Printed in the U.S.A.
ISBN 10 0-8307-6473-9 ISBN 13 978-0-8307-6473-0 gospellightvbs.com

Vacation Bible School

Join the stampede!

Vacation Bible School

Join the stampede!

© 2013 Gospel Light, Ventura, CA 93006. All rights reserved. Printed in the U.S.A.
ISBN 10 0-8307-6473-9 ISBN 13 978-0-8307-6473-0 gospellightvbs.com

SonWest ROUNDUP

Gospel Light's

A RIP-ROARING GOOD TIME WITH JESUS! **VBS**

Vacation Bible School

Join the stampede!

Gospel Light's

SonWest ROUNDUP

A RIP-ROARING GOOD TIME WITH JESUS! **VBS**

Vacation Bible School

Join the stampede!

© 2013 Gospel Light, Ventura, CA 93006. All rights reserved. Printed in the U.S.A.
ISBN 10 0-8307-6473-9 ISBN 13 978-0-8307-6473-0 gospellightvbs.com

Gospel Light's

SonWest ROUNDUP
A RIP-ROARING GOOD TIME WITH JESUS!
VBS

Vacation Bible School

Join the stampede!

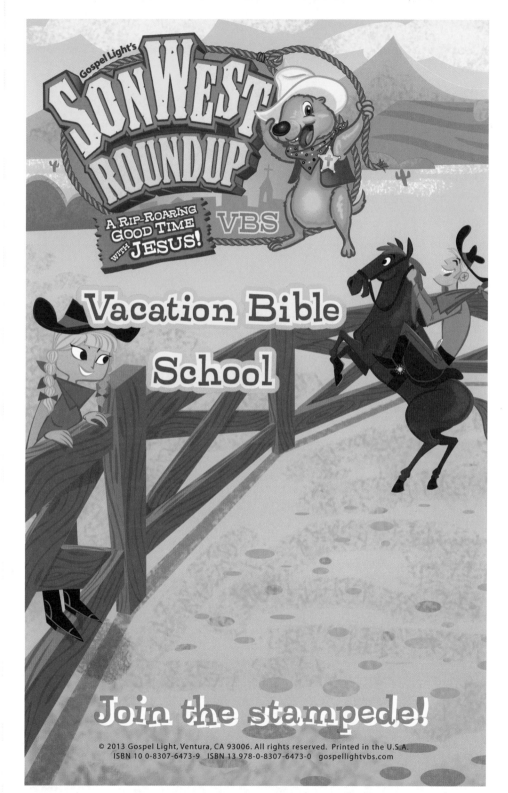

Gospel Light's

SonWest ROUNDUP
A RIP-ROARING GOOD TIME WITH JESUS!
VBS

Vacation Bible School

Join the stampede!

© 2013 Gospel Light, Ventura, CA 93006. All rights reserved. Printed in the U.S.A.
ISBN 10 0-8307-6473-9   ISBN 13 978-0-8307-6473-0   gospellightvbs.com

Gospel Light's
SonWest Roundup
A Rip-Roaring Good Time with Jesus! VBS

Vacation Bible School

Join the stampede!

Gospel Light's
SonWest Roundup
A Rip-Roaring Good Time with Jesus! VBS

Vacation Bible School

Join the stampede!

© 2013 Gospel Light, Ventura, CA 93006. All rights reserved. Printed in the U.S.A. ISBN 10 0-8307-6473-9 ISBN 13 978-0-8307-6473-0 gospellightvbs.com

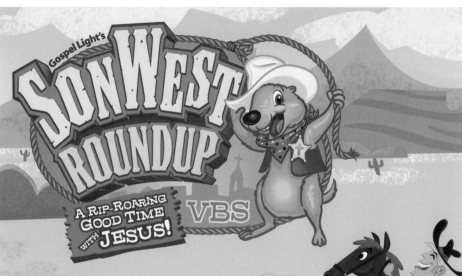

Vacation Bible School

Join the stampede!

Vacation Bible School

Join the stampede!

© 2013 Gospel Light, Ventura, CA 93006. All rights reserved. Printed in the U.S.A.
ISBN 10 0-8307-6473-9 ISBN 13 978-0-8307-6473-0 gospellightvbs.com

Vacation Bible School

Join the stampede!

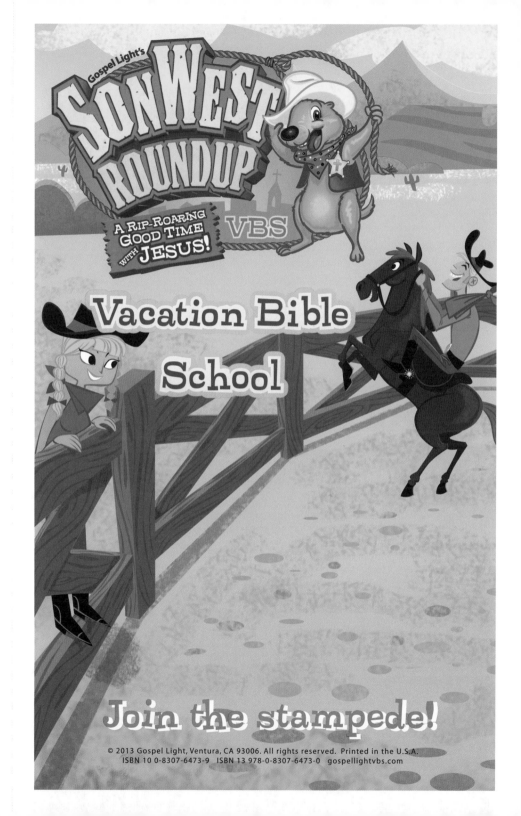

Gospel Light's SonWest Roundup VBS

A Rip-Roaring Good Time with Jesus!

Vacation Bible School

Join the stampede!

© 2013 Gospel Light, Ventura, CA 93006. All rights reserved. Printed in the U.S.A.
ISBN 10 0-8307-6473-9   ISBN 13 978-0-8307-6473-0   gospellightvbs.com

Vacation Bible School

Join the stampede!

Vacation Bible School

Join the stampede!

© 2013 Gospel Light, Ventura, CA 93006. All rights reserved. Printed in the U.S.A.
ISBN 10 0-8307-6473-9   ISBN 13 978-0-8307-6473-0   gospellightvbs.com

SonWest ROUNDUP

Gospel Light's

A RIP-ROARING GOOD TIME WITH JESUS! VBS

Vacation Bible School

Join the stampede!

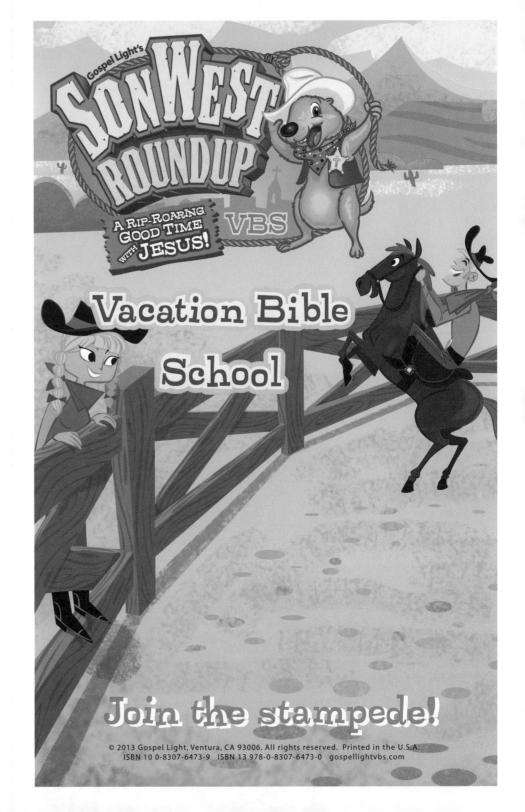

SonWest ROUNDUP

Gospel Light's

A RIP-ROARING GOOD TIME WITH JESUS! VBS

Vacation Bible School

Join the stampede!

© 2013 Gospel Light, Ventura, CA 93006. All rights reserved. Printed in the U.S.A.
ISBN 10 0-8307-6473-9 ISBN 13 978-0-8307-6473-0 gospellightvbs.com

Gospel Light's

SonWest ROUNDUP

A RIP-ROARING GOOD TIME WITH JESUS! **VBS**

Vacation Bible School

Join the stampede!

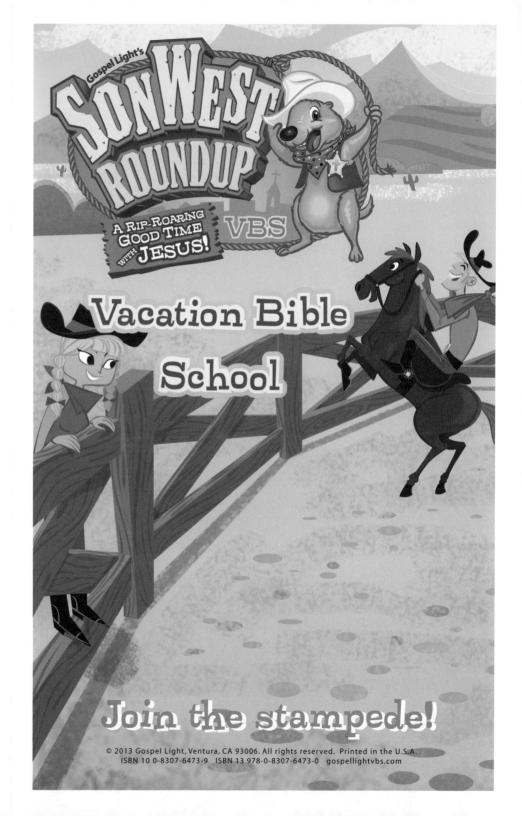

Gospel Light's

SonWest ROUNDUP

A RIP-ROARING GOOD TIME WITH JESUS! **VBS**

Vacation Bible School

Join the stampede!

© 2013 Gospel Light, Ventura, CA 93006. All rights reserved. Printed in the U.S.A.
ISBN 10 0-8307-6473-9 ISBN 13 978-0-8307-6473-0 gospellightvbs.com

SonWest ROUNDUP

Gospel Light's

A Rip-Roaring Good Time with Jesus! VBS

Vacation Bible School

Join the stampede!

Gospel Light's

SonWest ROUNDUP

A Rip-Roaring Good Time with Jesus! VBS

Vacation Bible School

Join the stampede!

© 2013 Gospel Light, Ventura, CA 93006. All rights reserved. Printed in the U.S.A.
ISBN 10 0-8307-6473-9   ISBN 13 978-0-8307-6473-0   gospellightvbs.com

Gospel Light's

SonWest ROUNDUP

A RIP-ROARING GOOD TIME WITH JESUS! VBS

Vacation Bible School

Join the stampede!

Gospel Light's

SonWest ROUNDUP

A RIP-ROARING GOOD TIME WITH JESUS! VBS

Vacation Bible School

Join the stampede!

© 2013 Gospel Light, Ventura, CA 93006. All rights reserved. Printed in the U.S.A.
ISBN 10 0-8307-6473-9 ISBN 13 978-0-8307-6473-0 gospellightvbs.com

Vacation Bible School

Join the stampede!

Vacation Bible School

Join the stampede!

© 2013 Gospel Light, Ventura, CA 93006. All rights reserved. Printed in the U.S.A.
ISBN 10 0-8307-6473-9   ISBN 13 978-0-8307-6473-0   gospellightvbs.com

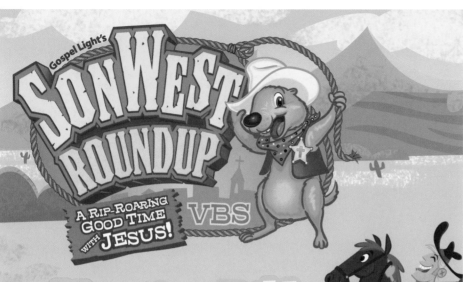

Vacation Bible School

Join the stampede!

Vacation Bible School

Join the stampede!

© 2013 Gospel Light, Ventura, CA 93006. All rights reserved. Printed in the U.S.A.
ISBN 10 0-8307-6473-9 ISBN 13 978-0-8307-6473-0 gospellightvbs.com

Gospel Light's

SonWest ROUNDUP

A RIP-ROARING GOOD TIME WITH JESUS! VBS

Vacation Bible School

Join the stampede!

Gospel Light's

SonWest ROUNDUP

A RIP-ROARING GOOD TIME WITH JESUS! VBS

Vacation Bible School

Join the stampede!

© 2013 Gospel Light, Ventura, CA 93006. All rights reserved. Printed in the U.S.A.
ISBN 10 0-8307-6473-9   ISBN 13 978-0-8307-6473-0   gospellightvbs.com

Vacation Bible School

Join the stampede!

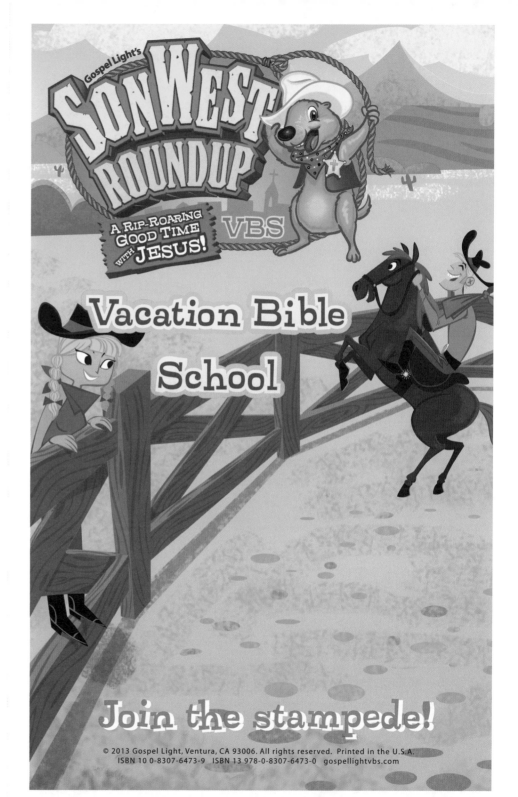

Vacation Bible School

Join the stampede!

© 2013 Gospel Light, Ventura, CA 93006. All rights reserved. Printed in the U.S.A.
ISBN 10 0-8307-6473-9 ISBN 13 978-0-8307-6473-0 gospellightvbs.com

Vacation Bible School

Join the stampede!

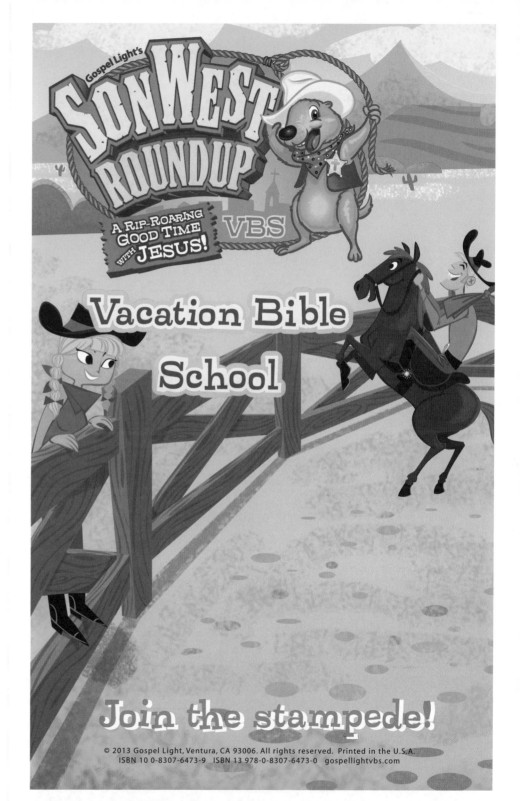

Vacation Bible School

Join the stampede!

© 2013 Gospel Light, Ventura, CA 93006. All rights reserved. Printed in the U.S.A.
ISBN 10 0-8307-6473-9 ISBN 13 978-0-8307-6473-0 gospellightvbs.com

Vacation Bible
School

Join the stampede!

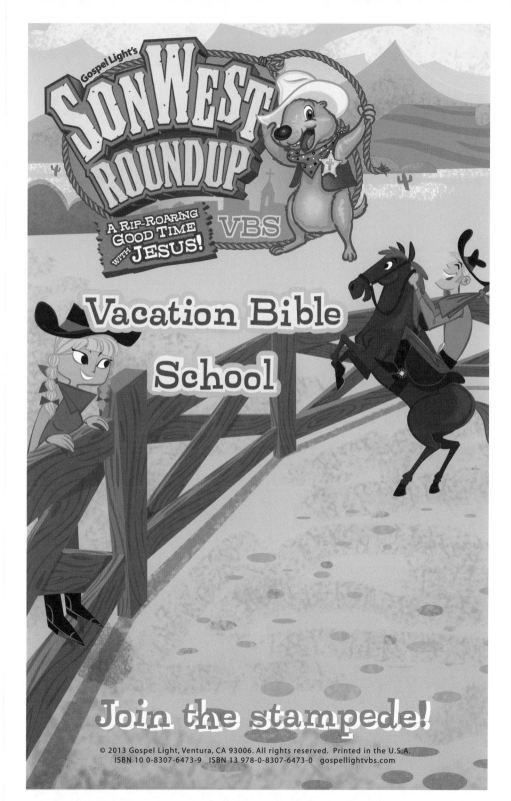

Vacation Bible
School

Join the stampede!

© 2013 Gospel Light, Ventura, CA 93006. All rights reserved. Printed in the U.S.A.
ISBN 10 0-8307-6473-9 ISBN 13 978-0-8307-6473-0 gospellightvbs.com

Vacation Bible School

Join the stampede!

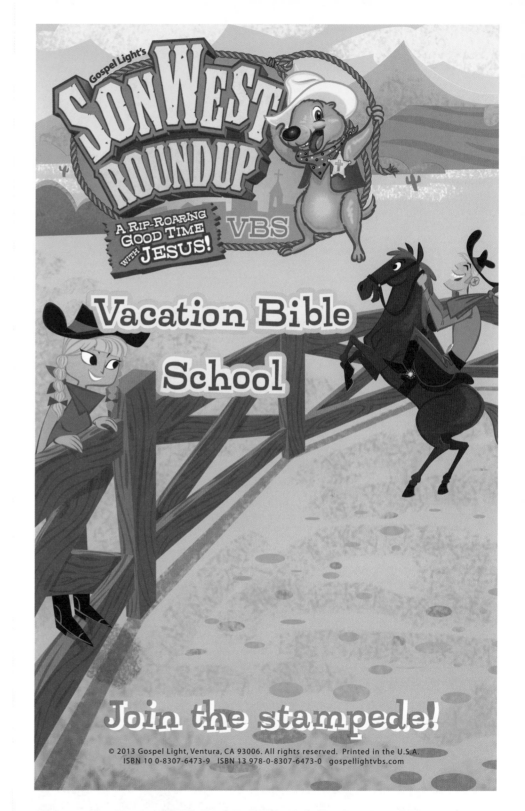

Vacation Bible School

Join the stampede!

© 2013 Gospel Light, Ventura, CA 93006. All rights reserved. Printed in the U.S.A.
ISBN 10 0-8307-6473-9   ISBN 13 978-0-8307-6473-0   gospellightvbs.com

Vacation Bible School

Join the stampede!

Vacation Bible School

Join the stampede!

© 2013 Gospel Light, Ventura, CA 93006. All rights reserved. Printed in the U.S.A.
ISBN 10 0-8307-6473-9   ISBN 13 978-0-8307-6473-0   gospellightvbs.com

Vacation Bible School

Join the stampede!

Vacation Bible School

Join the stampede!

© 2013 Gospel Light, Ventura, CA 93006. All rights reserved. Printed in the U.S.A.
ISBN 10 0-8307-6473-9   ISBN 13 978-0-8307-6473-0   gospellightvbs.com

Vacation Bible School

Join the stampede!

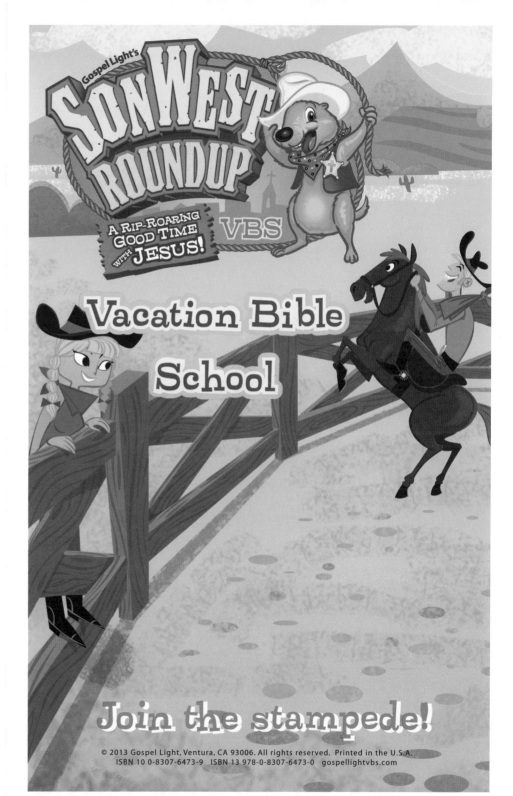

Gospel Light's

SonWest ROUNDUP

A RIP-ROARING GOOD TIME WITH JESUS! VBS

Vacation Bible School

Join the stampede!

© 2013 Gospel Light, Ventura, CA 93006. All rights reserved. Printed in the U.S.A.
ISBN 10 0-8307-6473-9   ISBN 13 978-0-8307-6473-0   gospellightvbs.com

Vacation Bible School

Join the stampede!

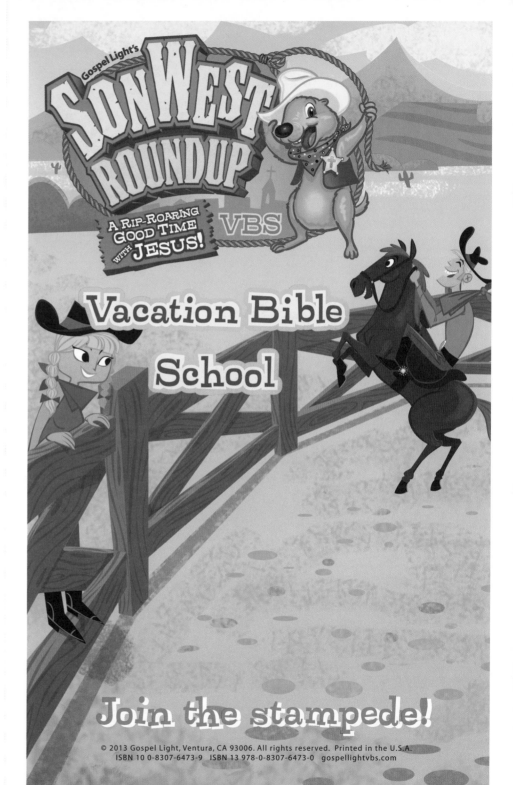

Vacation Bible School

Join the stampede!

© 2013 Gospel Light, Ventura, CA 93006. All rights reserved. Printed in the U.S.A.
ISBN 10 0-8307-6473-9 ISBN 13 978-0-8307-6473-0 gospellightvbs.com

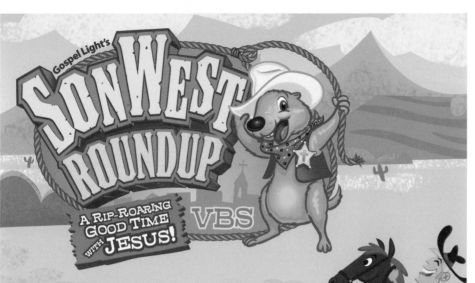

Vacation Bible School

Join the stampede!

Vacation Bible School

Join the stampede!

© 2013 Gospel Light, Ventura, CA 93006. All rights reserved. Printed in the U.S.A.
ISBN 10 0-8307-6473-9 ISBN 13 978-0-8307-6473-0 gospellightvbs.com

Vacation Bible School

Join the stampede!

Vacation Bible School

Join the stampede!

© 2013 Gospel Light, Ventura, CA 93006. All rights reserved. Printed in the U.S.A.
ISBN 10 0-8307-6473-9 ISBN 13 978-0-8307-6473-0 gospellightvbs.com

Vacation Bible School

Join the stampede!

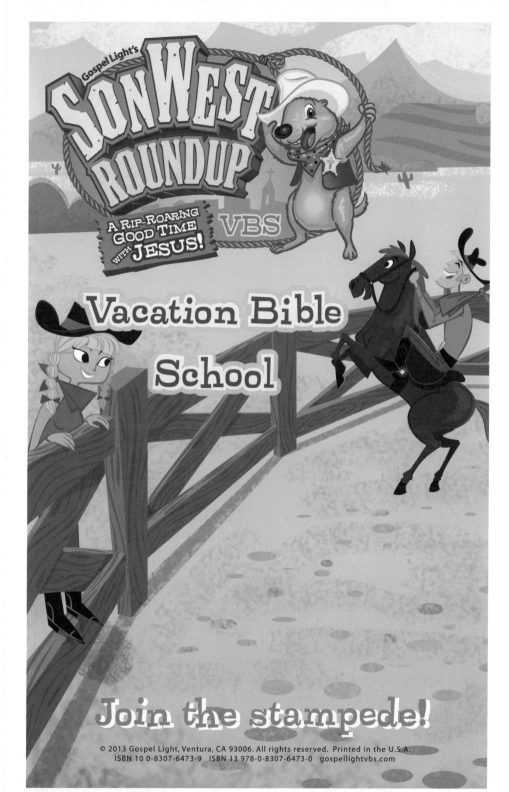

Vacation Bible School

Join the stampede!

© 2013 Gospel Light, Ventura, CA 93006. All rights reserved. Printed in the U.S.A.
ISBN 10 0-8307-6473-9   ISBN 13 978-0-8307-6473-0   gospellightvbs.com

Gospel Light's

SonWest ROUNDUP

A Rip-Roaring GOOD TIME with JESUS! VBS

Vacation Bible School

Join the stampede!

Gospel Light's

SonWest ROUNDUP

A Rip-Roaring GOOD TIME with JESUS! VBS

Vacation Bible School

Join the stampede!

© 2013 Gospel Light, Ventura, CA 93006. All rights reserved. Printed in the U.S.A.
ISBN 10 0-8307-6473-9   ISBN 13 978-0-8307-6473-0   gospellightvbs.com

Vacation Bible School

Join the stampede!

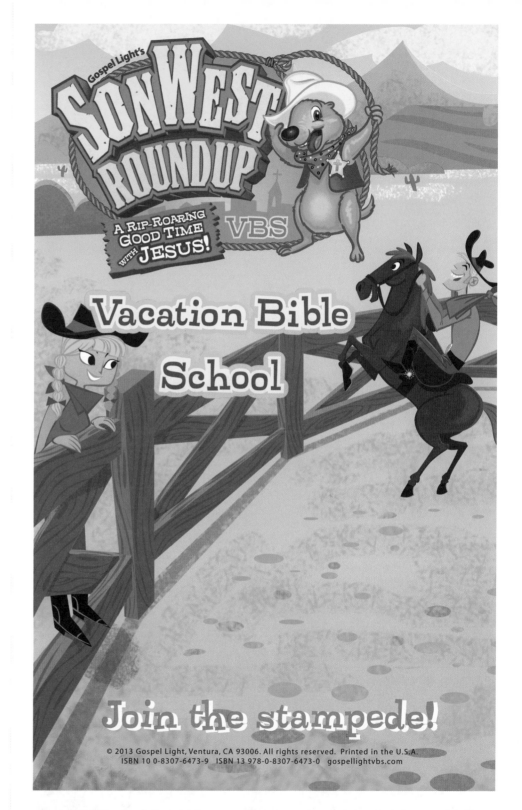

Gospel Light's
SonWest ROUNDUP
A RIP-ROARING GOOD TIME WITH JESUS! VBS

Vacation Bible School

Join the stampede!

© 2013 Gospel Light, Ventura, CA 93006. All rights reserved. Printed in the U.S.A.
ISBN 10 0-8307-6473-9   ISBN 13 978-0-8307-6473-0   gospellightvbs.com

Gospel Light's

SonWest ROUNDUP

A RIP-ROARING GOOD TIME WITH JESUS! VBS

Vacation Bible School

Join the stampede!

Vacation Bible School

Join the stampede!

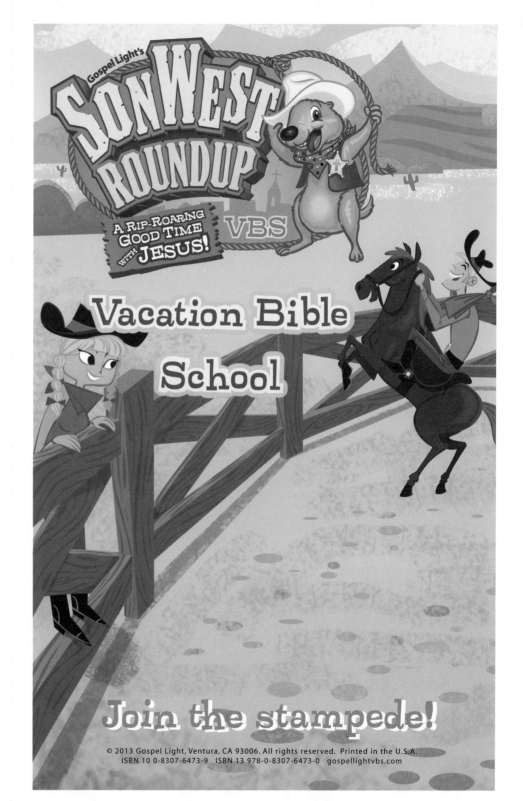

Vacation Bible School

Join the stampede!

© 2013 Gospel Light, Ventura, CA 93006. All rights reserved. Printed in the U.S.A.
ISBN 10 0-8307-6473-9   ISBN 13 978-0-8307-6473-0   gospellightvbs.com

Vacation Bible School

Join the stampede!

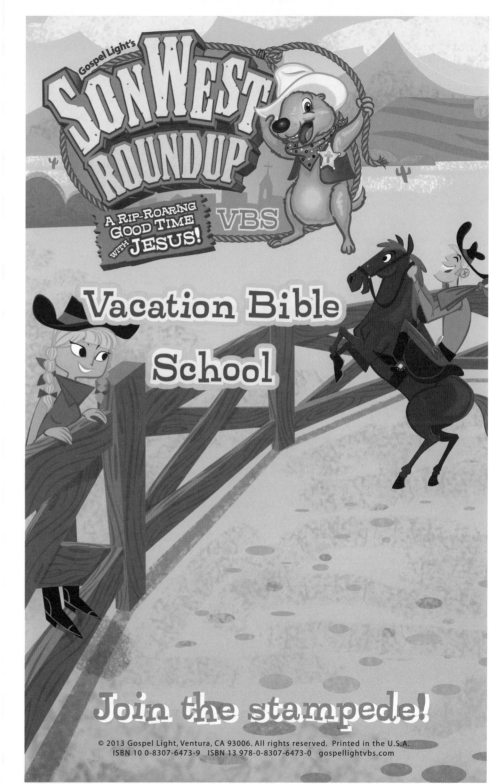

Vacation Bible School

Join the stampede!

© 2013 Gospel Light, Ventura, CA 93006. All rights reserved. Printed in the U.S.A.
ISBN 10 0-8307-6473-9   ISBN 13 978-0-8307-6473-0   gospellightvbs.com

Vacation Bible School

Join the stampede!

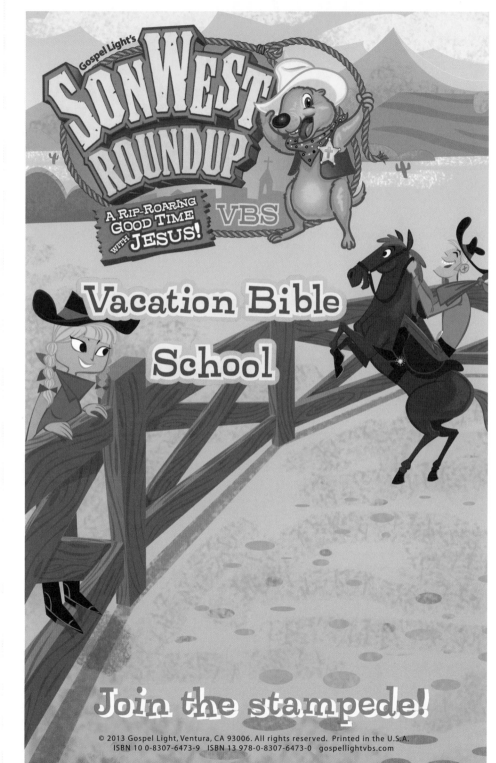

Vacation Bible School

Join the stampede!

© 2013 Gospel Light, Ventura, CA 93006. All rights reserved. Printed in the U.S.A.
ISBN 10 0-8307-6473-9   ISBN 13 978-0-8307-6473-0   gospellightvbs.com

Vacation Bible School

Join the stampede!

Vacation Bible School

Join the stampede!

© 2013 Gospel Light, Ventura, CA 93006. All rights reserved. Printed in the U.S.A.
ISBN 10 0-8307-6473-9   ISBN 13 978-0-8307-6473-0   gospellightvbs.com

SonWest ROUNDUP

A RIP-ROARING GOOD TIME WITH JESUS! VBS

Vacation Bible School

Join the stampede!

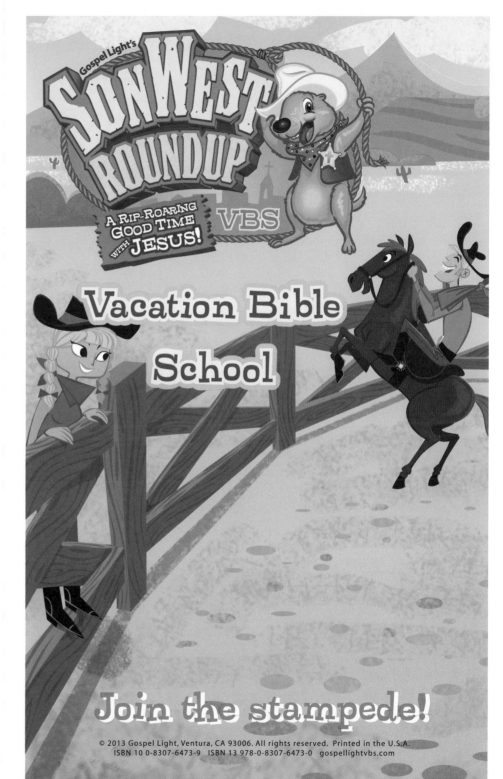

SonWest ROUNDUP

A RIP-ROARING GOOD TIME WITH JESUS! VBS

Vacation Bible School

Join the stampede!

© 2013 Gospel Light, Ventura, CA 93006. All rights reserved. Printed in the U.S.A.
ISBN 10 0-8307-6473-9 ISBN 13 978-0-8307-6473-0 gospellightvbs.com

Vacation Bible School

Join the stampede!

Vacation Bible School

Join the stampede!

© 2013 Gospel Light, Ventura, CA 93006. All rights reserved. Printed in the U.S.A.
ISBN 10 0-8307-6473-9   ISBN 13 978-0-8307-6473-0   gospellightvbs.com

Vacation Bible School

Join the stampede!

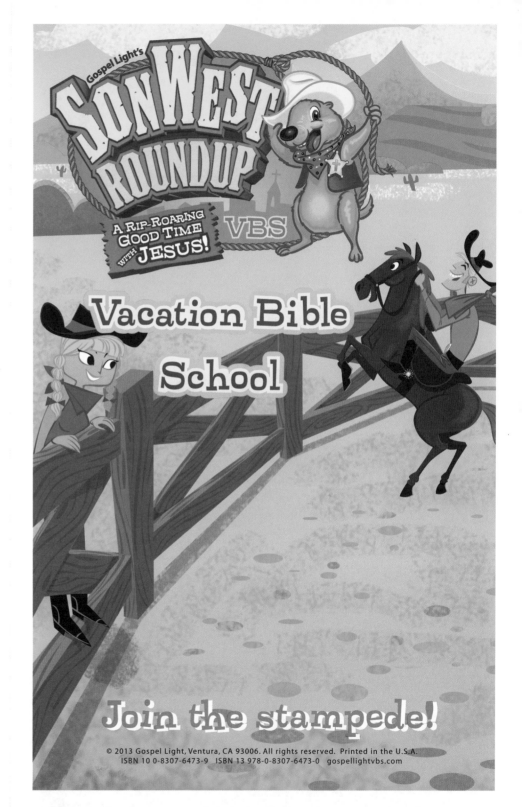

Vacation Bible School

Join the stampede!

© 2013 Gospel Light, Ventura, CA 93006. All rights reserved. Printed in the U.S.A.
ISBN 10 0-8307-6473-9   ISBN 13 978-0-8307-6473-0   gospellightvbs.com

Vacation Bible School

Join the stampede!

Vacation Bible School

Join the stampede!

© 2013 Gospel Light, Ventura, CA 93006. All rights reserved. Printed in the U.S.A.
ISBN 10 0-8307-6473-9   ISBN 13 978-0-8307-6473-0   gospellightvbs.com

Vacation Bible School

Join the stampede!

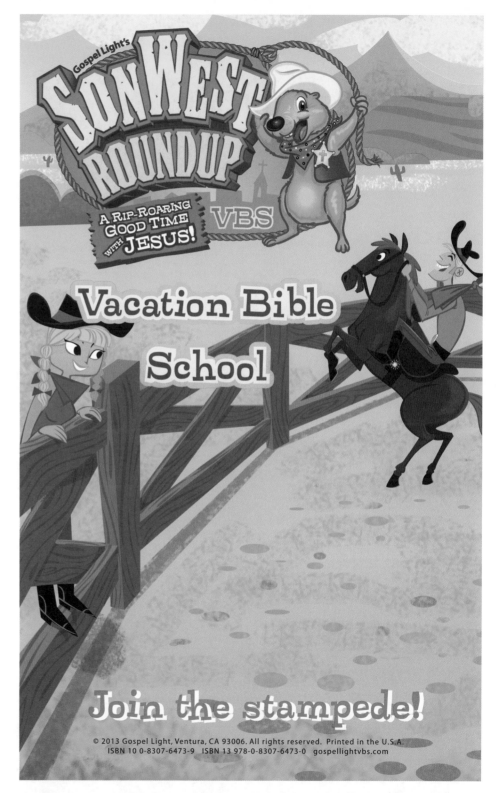

Vacation Bible School

Join the stampede!

© 2013 Gospel Light, Ventura, CA 93006. All rights reserved. Printed in the U.S.A.
ISBN 10 0-8307-6473-9 ISBN 13 978-0-8307-6473-0 gospellightvbs.com

Gospel Light's

SonWest ROUNDUP

A RIP-ROARING GOOD TIME WITH JESUS! **VBS**

Vacation Bible School

Join the stampede!

ISBN 10 0-8307-6473-9   ISBN 13 978-0-8307-6473-0   gospellightvbs.com

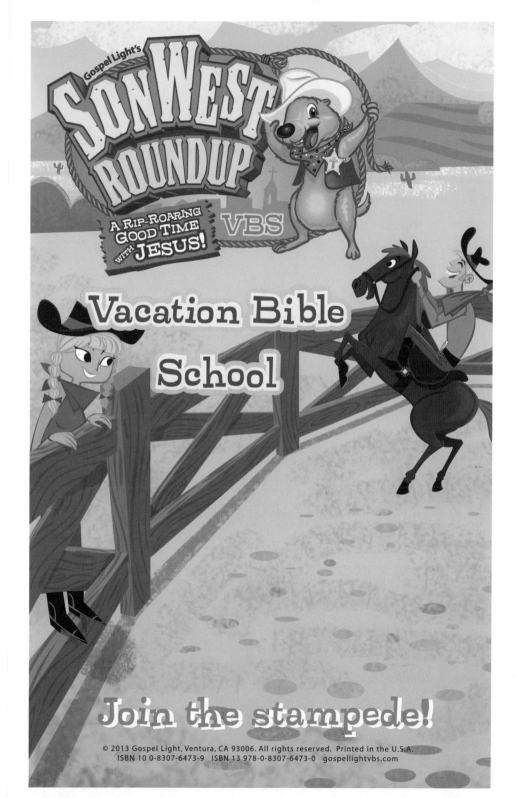

Gospel Light's

SonWest ROUNDUP

A RIP-ROARING GOOD TIME WITH JESUS! **VBS**

Vacation Bible School

Join the stampede!

© 2013 Gospel Light, Ventura, CA 93006. All rights reserved. Printed in the U.S.A.
ISBN 10 0-8307-6473-9   ISBN 13 978-0-8307-6473-0   gospellightvbs.com

Vacation Bible School

Join the stampede!

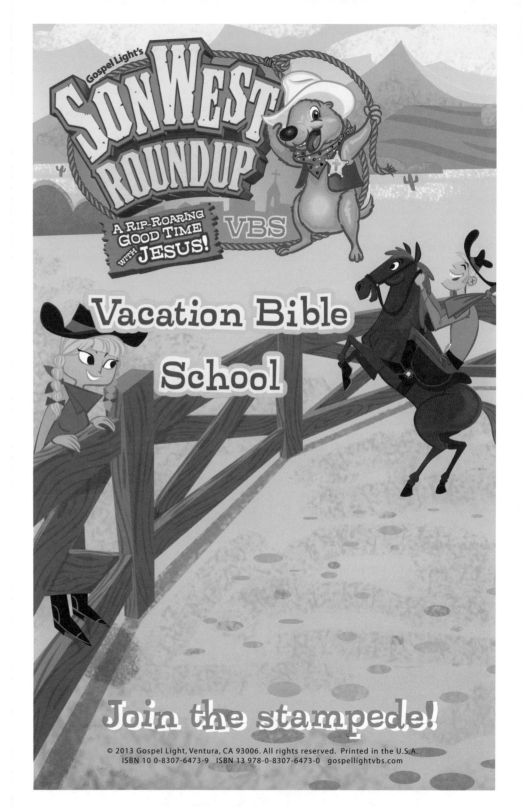

Vacation Bible School

Join the stampede!

© 2013 Gospel Light, Ventura, CA 93006. All rights reserved. Printed in the U.S.A.
ISBN 10 0-8307-6473-9   ISBN 13 978-0-8307-6473-0   gospellightvbs.com

Vacation Bible School

Join the stampede!

Vacation Bible School

Join the stampede!

© 2013 Gospel Light, Ventura, CA 93006. All rights reserved. Printed in the U.S.A.
ISBN 10 0-8307-6473-9 ISBN 13 978-0-8307-6473-0 gospellightvbs.com

Vacation Bible School

Join the stampede!

Vacation Bible School

Join the stampede!

© 2013 Gospel Light, Ventura, CA 93006. All rights reserved. Printed in the U.S.A.
ISBN 10 0-8307-6473-9 ISBN 13 978-0-8307-6473-0 gospellightvbs.com

Vacation Bible School

Join the stampede!

Vacation Bible School

Join the stampede!

© 2013 Gospel Light, Ventura, CA 93006. All rights reserved. Printed in the U.S.A.
ISBN 10 0-8307-6473-9 ISBN 13 978-0-8307-6473-0 gospellightvbs.com

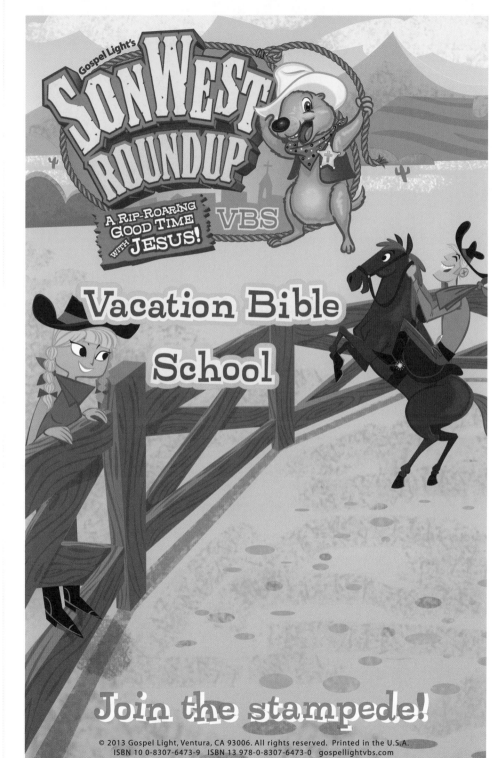

© 2013 Gospel Light, Ventura, CA 93006. All rights reserved. Printed in the U.S.A.
ISBN 10 0-8307-6473-9   ISBN 13 978-0-8307-6473-0   gospellightvbs.com

SonWest Roundup

A Rip-Roaring Good Time with Jesus!

VBS

Gospel Light's

Vacation Bible School

Join the stampede!

SonWest Roundup

A Rip-Roaring Good Time with Jesus!

VBS

Gospel Light's

Vacation Bible School

Join the stampede!

© 2013 Gospel Light, Ventura, CA 93006. All rights reserved. Printed in the U.S.A.
ISBN 10 0-8307-6473-9   ISBN 13 978-0-8307-6473-0   gospellightvbs.com

Vacation Bible School

Join the stampede!

Vacation Bible School

Join the stampede!

© 2013 Gospel Light, Ventura, CA 93006. All rights reserved. Printed in the U.S.A.
ISBN 10 0-8307-6473-9 ISBN 13 978-0-8307-6473-0 gospellightvbs.com

SonWest ROUNDUP

Gospel Light's

A RIP-ROARING GOOD TIME WITH JESUS! VBS

Vacation Bible School

Join the stampede!

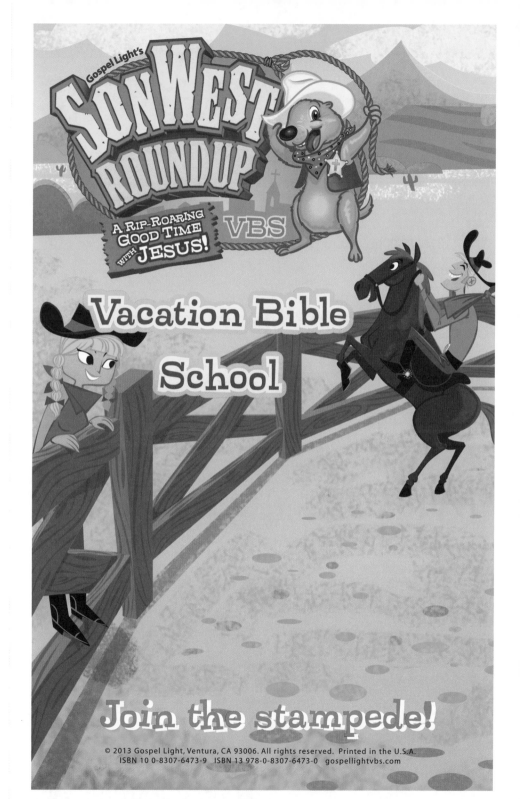

SonWest ROUNDUP

Gospel Light's

A RIP-ROARING GOOD TIME WITH JESUS! VBS

Vacation Bible School

Join the stampede!

© 2013 Gospel Light, Ventura, CA 93006. All rights reserved. Printed in the U.S.A.
ISBN 10 0-8307-6473-9 ISBN 13 978-0-8307-6473-0 gospellightvbs.com

Vacation Bible School

Join the stampede!

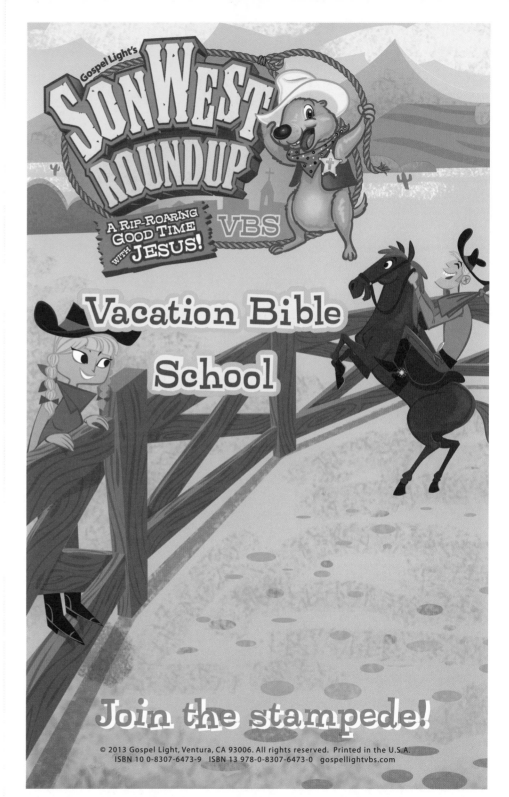

Vacation Bible School

Join the stampede!

© 2013 Gospel Light, Ventura, CA 93006. All rights reserved. Printed in the U.S.A.
ISBN 10 0-8307-6473-9   ISBN 13 978-0-8307-6473-0   gospellightvbs.com